ANSWERS TO THE 50 MOST IMPORTANT QUESTIONS ABOUT PRIVATE MENTAL HEALTH PRACTICE

About the Authors

Bruce D. Forman received his Ph.D. from Duke University in 1978. He completed a post-doctoral fellowship in research at the Missouri Institute of Psychiatry. Dr. Forman has held Faculty positions at the University of South Dakota School of Medicine and at the University of Miami. Dr. Forman was Associate Professor of Counseling Psychology and directed the program in Marriage and Family Therapy at the University of Miami. He held joint appointments in the Department of Psychiatry and the Department of Family and Community Medicine. He was in part-time private practice until 1993, and has been full time since then. Dr. Forman is an Approved Supervisor and Fellow of the American Association for Marriage and Family Therapy. He serves on the editorial boards of two psychotherapy journals and has authored over 50 articles and chapters in scientific and professional journals and books. He has coauthored two books on professional mental health practice.

Wade H. Silverman received his Ph.D. from Kent State University in 1969. He was a member of the faculty in the Department of Psychiatry at the University of Illinois-Chicago. Dr. Silverman then served as Professor and Head of the Psychology Division at Emory University School of Medicine and was Chair of the Department of Psychology at Barry University. He has been in full-time independent practice since 1992 and was Visiting Professor in Nova Southeastern University's School of Psychology. Dr. Silverman is a Diplomate in Clinical Psychology, American Board of Professional Psychology, Fellow of the Academy of Clinical Psychology, and a Fellow of four divisions of the American Psychological Association. He is President-Elect of APA's Division of Psychotherapy and has served as Editor of Psychotherapy: Theory, Research, Practice, and Training since 1994. Dr. Silverman has written or presented over 100 articles and papers on psychotherapy, substance abuse, and health psychology in addition to two books.

ANSWERS TO THE 50 MOST IMPORTANT QUESTIONS ABOUT PRIVATE MENTAL HEALTH PRACTICE

By

BRUCE D. FORMAN, Ph.D.

and

WADE H. SILVERMAN, Ph.D.

CHARLES C THOMAS • PUBLISHER, LTD.
Springfield • Illinois • U.S.A.

Published and Distributed Throughout the World by
CHARLES C THOMAS • PUBLISHER, LTD.
2600 South First Street
Springfield, Illinois 62794-9265

©1998 by CHARLES C THOMAS • PUBLISHER, LTD.
ISBN 0-398-06887-9 (paper)

Library of Congress Catalog Card Number: 98-8151

With THOMAS BOOKS *careful attention is given to all details of manufacturing and design. It is the Publisher's desire to present books that are satisfactory as to their physical qualities and artistic possibilities and appropriate for their particular use.* THOMAS BOOKS *will be true to those laws of quality that assure a good name and good will.*

Printed in the United States of America

SM-R-3

Library of Congress Cataloging-in-Publication Data

Forman, Bruce D.
      Answers to the 50 most important questions about private mental
      health practice / by Bruce D. Forman and Wade H. Silverman
            p.   cm.
      Includes bibliographical references and index.
      ISBN 0-398-06887-9 (pbk.).
      1. Psychotherapy–Practice. 2. Psychiatry–Practice.–United States.
I. Silverman, Wade H. II. Title.
RC465.5.F66 1998
616.89'0068–dc21   98-8151
                                                                                            CIP

This book is dedicated to the memory of
Douglas R. Rogers (1949-1997)

PREFACE

We began work on this book by polling 25 graduate students in psychology along with 25 experienced, full-time practicing psychologists, psychiatrists, social workers, mental health counselors, and marriage & family therapists for their opinions concerning private practice. Specifically, we asked for questions they would like to have answered or questions they believed to be most important for those who are either beginning, or are already in practice. Some of the questions we received appeared so simple at first blush that we began to realize how much basic knowledge about professional practice is missing in graduate curricula. We hope that this set of questions, along with answers, will be useful to anyone who offers private mental health services.

Because the arena for private practice is influenced by the changing tides of political, economic, and social trends, significant issues for practitioners are continuously changing. For that reason, we cannot be as thorough as you might desire. Or, we may have missed some essential issues about which you have questions. Not to worry, simply communicate them to us and we will address them in a future volume.

B. D. F.
W. H. S.

A Note of Caution

Nothing in this book is intended, nor should be construed as legal counsel, managerial advice, or any other professional service. If legal advice is sought, the reader is advised to consult an attorney. Specific business information or suggestions should be obtained from a qualified practice management consultant.

CONTENTS

ANSWERS TO THE 50 MOST IMPORTANT QUESTIONS ABOUT PRIVATE MENTAL HEALTH PRACTICE

Question 1

How will I know if private practice is right for me?

Answer

Private practice is not right for everyone. Particularly for those who have graduated from a scientist/practitioner or public service model training program, the private practice setting is quite foreign. It is much more like a business setting than an academic setting. Before you choose such a career, you should take an inventory of your values, your desires, and your temperament. To succeed as a private practitioner you must be entrepreneurial, ready to take financial risks, able to work without supervision, survive in isolation, have a high tolerance for ambiguity, have a support system, have sufficient savings to cover living costs for six months or longer, be confident in your clinical skills, have a referral network, possess a standing in the community as a competent professional, have the ability to handle lack of structure, be comfortable without a regular paycheck, be a self-starter, be organized about records and finances, and be knowledgeable about the local market. This is a tall order, particularly if you also have the responsibilities of a family.

Only you can judge how well you measure up to these criteria and how prepared you are to accept the risks. It is important that you are comfortable with this decision because it is very difficult to practice this craft successfully under too much personal stress. On the other hand, if you are driven by strong needs to be autonomous, then this is the prime choice for a career for you. Edmund Cava, MD, in private practice for over 40 years says there is an old Italian saying: "*Emeglio essere proprietario di una barca, che capitano di una nave*" which translated into English is: "It is better to have your own rowboat than it is to be the captain on someone else's yacht." If this strikes a familiar chord for you, perhaps you are someone who simply must go into private practice to satisfy your need for independence and personal ambitions.

Question 2

What degree/credentials are needed to enter private practice?

Answer

There are people in private practice who have no degrees or credentials whatsoever and are practicing in perfectly legal ways. Such individuals do not use titles that are regulated, nor can they receive third-party payments for their services or participate in managed care provider networks. All U.S. states and Canadian provinces have laws governing titles such as "psychologist" and "psychotherapist." With few exceptions, psychologists are required to hold doctoral degrees (i.e., PhD/PsyD, EdD) from programs that are either accredited by the American Psychological Association, or are organized in a fashion similar to one that is accredited. All but two states in the U.S. have laws that govern clinical social workers, 40 states have legislation regulating mental health or professional counselors, and 38 states have credentialing for marriage and family therapists. There has been a trend over the past decade or so to have laws enacted which provide for the regulation of these psychotherapy disciplines. Several organizations (e.g., National Association of Social Workers; National Association of Certified Mental Health Counselors) have standards and procedures for granting designation to those with advanced levels of experience. For someone who is unsure about what the laws are in a particular state, it is best to check with state regulatory agencies or licensing boards *before* entering private practice. This could prevent unwanted problems that might be costly, as well as potentially damaging to one's reputation.

It is often possible to be employed at organized service settings like mental health centers or family service agencies without being licensed. Many private practitioners started their careers by working in such facilities until they received enough experience to become licensed. An advantage to obtaining licensure is that it opens the door to eligibility for third-party payments from health insurance carriers and managed care organizations. That is the main reason why professional associations usually advocate for what is called freedom-of-choice legislation. This mandates the right of the consumer of mental health services to choose *any* licensed professional practitioner of such services in his/her state irrespective of professional training. Historically, some insurance companies recognized only an MD for third party eligibility. Similarly, most professions provide state licensure/certification/registration of their discipline.

Question 3

What experience is needed to enter private practice?

Answer

Those people who have decided on psychotherapy as a career are required to have supervised clinical experience as part of their graduate training. Furthermore, professionals in most states must have licenses to practice. As part of the application process those who register must also document that they received postgraduate clinical supervision by one or more supervisors who, themselves, were appropriately credentialed. In spite of all these requirements, no one is ever fully prepared upon graduation and after internship or postgraduate supervision to be a fully-qualified therapist. This is why most states, and all national professional organizations, require documentation of continuing education experiences.

In addition to acquiring clinical competence with a wide range of problems and populations, it is also a good idea to know about the business side of the profession. Unless you decide to work for someone else, you must acquire competencies needed for running a small business. These include office management, public relations, accounting, marketing, tax planning, and financial management.

It is also important to note that the typical individual who enters private practice does not do so immediately upon receiving her/his degree. She/he has usually had several years of clinical experience working in someone else's organized practice setting, in a public agency, or in a private for-profit institution. Most therapists begin work on a part-time basis and gradually work into full-time private practice.

Question 4

How much money can I expect to earn in private practice?

Answer

In a survey by *Psychotherapy Finances*, published in 1990, it was found that the median annual income for full-time psychotherapists practicing in the U.S. was $62,700. Psychologists earned approximately $73,100, social workers earned $53,200, and family therapists earned $50,000. A similar survey was conducted in 1996, with 1000 private practitioners, and reported in *Practice Strategies*. These results indicated that things had not changed dramatically. Of all therapists in either full- or part-time private practice, 67 percent earned $50,000, or less, annually. Over 80 percent of those earning $25,000, or less, annually had income from other sources. Annual practice revenues of $75,000, or greater, were reported for 53 percent of psychologists, 20 percent of social workers, 16 percent of family therapists, and 14 percent of professional counselors. Thirty-one percent of all psychologists surveyed reported annual practice revenues of at least $100,000. While this gives a picture of the possibilities, in 1996, more than half the therapists in each profession indicated that their overall practice incomes dropped between 5 percent and 15 percent over the preceding two years.

In the 1990 report, the median fee for individual sessions was $80 and for group therapy it was $40. In the 1996 report, the median fees were $82 for individual therapy and $43 for group therapy. Naturally, there is a range in fees that are actually charged. These vary by both profession and geographic region. Fees tended to be highest in the northeastern and western areas of the U.S.

For individual therapy, fees were at least $100 for 47 percent of psychologists. Just over 50 percent of social workers, 63 percent of family therapists, and 57 percent of professional counselors had individual therapy usual, customary, and reasonable (UCR) rates ranging from $75 to $100. It is worth noting that most practitioners have a sliding fee scale, generally ranging from a 10 to 15 percent discount of their UCR. This is relatively close to the negotiated discount for managed care, which averages 16 percent of UCR, but can be considerably higher. For instance, the 1996 average fee for psychologists was $99 nationally, but managed care paid psychologists an average of $70, or a 29 percent discount, for individual therapy. Interestingly, managed care accounted for about one-third of the private practice income for all psychotherapists. It was unclear just how many hours each week were devoted to earning one-third of the revenues.

Question 5

What are the advantages and disadvantages of being in private practice?

Answer

As previously noted, there are a host of reasons why individuals decide on private practice as a career, the most important of which is independence. We often hear that the "American Dream" is for someone to own his/her own business, instead of being an employee for someone else. What this means for a psychotherapist is that you set your own schedule, decide what you will charge for your services, and determine how long and how hard you will work. Many clinicians we know love their work so much they claim they actually feel energized at the end of a long day. They relate to the richness of working directly with the patient/clients' perceptions of their experiences and are rewarded by helping them. These therapists are inspired by their patient/clients' struggles. There are also practical advantages to this career. A clinician who is also a good business person can make a nice living.

On the negative side, many clinicians complain about how competitive their profession has become. Some therapists say their time is not their own or they have lost the sense of freedom they had when they first entered private practice. This is because clinicians are now required to keep detailed notes, complete treatment plans, and petition insurance carriers and managed care organizations for patient/client visits. Some of these entities require a recycling of all these activities every fifth session. Another factor is the increase in litigation activity requiring mental health professionals to be in constant contact with their office. They have to carry their profession with them everywhere in the form of beepers or cellular phones, so as to be accessible to existing and prospective patient/clients.

Also, many clinicians are uncomfortable with collections. They do not like to ask for overdue payments from patients/clients, particularly when they are aware of their financial reversals. There are a myriad of difficulties associated with collecting payments from Health Maintenance Organizations (HMOs), Preferred Provider Organizations (PPOs), and other third-party payers. Many practitioners report a precipitous drop of usual and customary fees and increased difficulty in obtaining payments. Demands for more detailed documentation of services for reimbursement or utilization review have increased exponentially.

Practitioners must now spend many extra hours completing paperwork or speaking directly with case managers, thus reducing billable contact hours available for patients/clients. Consequently, it is more difficult to get compensated for work than it was just a few years ago. It has been very difficult for full-time private practitioners to manage their practices without support staff. This adds to the overhead costs.

Question 6

Is it possible to keep my full-time job and start private practice on a part-time basis?

Answer

It is very risky to start any new business venture, particularly one that is as labor intensive as mental health practice, without financial backup. A typical practice requires many months, or even years to build. So, starting part-time is usually the most prudent option. A common way to accomplish this is for the individual to keep his/her full-time position while building the practice on evenings and weekends. One avenue of opportunity is to contact busy practitioners or group practices. They often refer their overflow to therapists who are willing to pay an administrative fee for sharing overhead expenses. Other arrangements can include compensation on an hourly or percentage-of-collections basis. As a contract employee, you are more likely to build a referral base because your name will be more widely recognized. Whether or not you choose to establish your own full-time practice, or first work with others, practice building requires intensive efforts in marketing.

Question 7

Can masters-level practitioners compete with MDs and PhDs in the private arena?

Answer

Masters-level practitioners have been giving psychologists and other doctoral-level providers significant competition for many years. However, the masters-level therapist has several major limitations to success. The first is the manner in which the public and the other professions perceive MDs and PhDs/PsyDs. Since they undergo a longer period of training, MDs and PhDs/PsyDs are assumed to be more skilled and more highly educated than masters-level practitioners. Indeed they are – however, training does not necessarily translate into clinical skills. There are highly competent practitioners at all levels of training and experience. In addition, many of the requirements in doctoral programs or medical schools are not relevant to psychotherapeutic priorities. They include research methods, statistics, and general psychology. Most psychiatric residencies spend little time focusing on systems of psychotherapy theory and practice or even developing sophisticated therapeutic skills. Rather, they emphasize pharmaceutical approaches. The amount of training in developing therapeutic skills may be similar in masters and doctoral level programs. This is not an indictment of psychology or psychiatry, only a comment about the differences in training. As an example, the art and science of psychiatry demand the mastery of biological approaches. Keeping up with advances in psychopharmacology requires considerable time that could be applied to learning psychotherapeutic skills. There is also an economic disincentive for psychiatrists to perform psychotherapy, since other commonly used procedure codes (e.g., medication management) can result in more patients seen per hour, with a concomitant higher hourly income.

A second major limitation to practicing with a terminal masters degree is the relative lack of recognition by third-party payers. Even in those states that have freedom-of-choice legislation, that choice does not always extend to masters-level practitioners. Finally, the managed care movement has officially relegated masters-level clinicians to second-class citizenship by formally establishing a fee schedule that is significantly lower than doctoral level payment.

Question 8

What are the requirements for licensing mental health practitioners? Is there reciprocity among states?

Answer

Currently, forty states require licensure for mental health counselors, and 48 states and the District of Columbia license social workers. There are licensing or certification laws for psychologists in all 50 states. According to the American Association for Marriage and Family Therapy, marriage and family therapists must be licensed in 38 states, and that number is growing. Licensure or certification usually requires completion of specified courses and a required number of hours under the supervision of a duly licensed, or otherwise credentialed, professional.

There is not much consistency, and therefore not much cooperation, across states or disciplines regarding reciprocal licensing. Thus, a practitioner moving from one state to another may be faced with a long list of requirements that must be completed in order to obtain another license. This can be very frustrating for the therapist who has qualified for licensure and practiced for many years to be rejected for licensure in a neighboring state. In addition, state bureaucracies can be slow and disorganized in the handling of petitions for licensing. We have heard many horror stories about lost paperwork, employee intransigence, or disrespectful examiners.

One of our favorite stories is one that began in a typical fashion but ended quite remarkably. It happened in the 1970s, when a psychologist we know decided to semi-retire and move to Florida. He applied for licensure by reciprocity since he held a license in another state and was also a Diplomate of the American Board of Professional Psychology. Upon being informed by the board that he would have to sit for an oral examination, this psychologist decided he would do some homework on the law. He found out that as an examinee he had the right to examine board members on their areas of expertise, as defined by their doctoral dissertations. He then wrote to the board to inform them that he was going to exercise this right at his oral examination. The next communication to him was a letter proclaiming the board's decision to grant him a Florida license without examination.

Question 9

Do practitioners really need malpractice insurance? If so, how much?

Answer

There is some debate over whether mental health practitioners should carry malpractice insurance. Bennett et al. (1990) advocate for almost universal purchase of malpractice insurance including academics, researchers, and agency employees, as well as private practitioners. Their reasoning is twofold. Professional work is complex, making one vulnerable to second-guessing. Second, accessing the legal system is easy and many people use this threat to harass and irritate. Other professionals argue the opposite. Forman (1990/1991) and Turkington (1986) take the position that concern with lawsuits is overstated. The probability of any practitioner being targeted for a malpractice suit is infinitesimally small. The choice is yours. In either case, whether you choose to purchase protection or not, it is essential to take a proactive stance and avoid malpractice. An excellent resource to taking preventative measures is Bob Woody's *Fifty Ways to Avoid Malpractice* (1988).

Irrespective of your philosophical position, these are the realities of the marketplace that may force a decision. You cannot obtain privileges at hospitals nor practice in most HMOs, PPOs, and provider networks without malpractice insurance. Sometimes the minimum amount required is specified on applications for hospital privileges or network membership as part of the credentialing process. Commonly, this is set at $1,000,000 per claim and $1,000,000 aggregate. Not all policies are the same, however. An important distinction is between "claims-made" and "occurrence-based" policies. VandeCreek (1990) explains that an occurrence-based policy is one that covers claims that were made *at the time the alleged misconduct occurred.* By contrast, a claims-made policy covers claims only *so long as the policy is in force.* The occurrence-based policy is therefore preferable for broad-based protection, whereas the claims-made policy is more economical. You can also obtain a special policy called a "tail" to add to your claims-made policy so as to provide retroactive coverage when your policy is no longer in force.

Question 10

What resources are needed to start a practice? How much will it cost?

Answer

Resources depend on the type and scale of practice that you desire. You can start on a shoestring budget with just a few essentials. First, you must have a place to see patients/clients. You can lease an office or begin by working out of your home. While this can save on costs, it might also disrupt your personal and family life. As an alternative to working out of your home, you may be able to negotiate use of an office at your current place of employment. Or, you may decide to sublet space on a part-time basis. Arrangements for subletting include fixed monthly rent for a specified number of hours or may be based on actual use. For example, one therapist sublets an office from a colleague for part-time use. She pays her colleague $15 per hour of use. Another therapist has an office in one section of an urban county but has a number of patients in another part of the county. He arranged to use space in a group medical practice office for $300 per month. Irrespective of where you decide to work, you must ensure the confidentiality of your patient/clients. This requires attention to soundproofing, a discrete waiting room arrangement, and door locks.

You will also require furniture for your office. Bargains abound at second-hand furniture stores. Fundamentally, all you need is a place for therapist and patients/clients to sit with sufficient lighting. How your office is appointed is a matter of personal taste. However, how your office is decorated is an essential feature of your image.

For most beginners, their primary concern is getting referrals and using income for basic operational costs. Any surplus should then be used for practice expansion.

Office communication is an essential aspect of practice particularly for emergencies and referrals. In addition to an answering machine and pager, you may want to have voice mail. Other essentials include an appointment book, a supply of documents for record keeping and billing, a checking account, stationary, and business cards.

As your practice grows, so does your overhead. You may require your own suite of offices to accommodate a secretary, a therapy group, and an assessment area. Low cost furniture may be replaced with plush decor that is professionally appointed by an interior designer. The telephone can be expanded to a sophisticated voice mail system that activates therapists' beepers. As your practice becomes more successful, you may need to hire an accountant to handle tax matters, as well as a marketing/public relations consultant. Also, as the practice volume of business increases, it may be cost-effective to purchase a computer system to manage patient information and billing. There are a number of commercially available software programs for practice management that can be had for just a few hundred dollars. Some that are worth checking into include Office Therapy (1-800-887-2455), Shrink-for-Windows (1-800-456-3003), Therapist Helper (1-800-343-5737), Practice Magic (1-510-528-7000), The Therapist (1-800-895-3344), and SumTime (1-800-767-5788).

Question 11

What is the status of hospital privileges for nonphysicians?

Answer

Mental health professionals throughout the U.S. have asserted their rights toward parity with psychiatry in terms of delivering mental health services. Nowhere has this been more successful than in the case of hospital privileges. In 1990, the California Supreme Court ruled that a hospital may permit clinical psychologists to provide psychological services without discriminating restrictions. This decision overturned the 1988 California Court of Appeals ruling. Previously it was the custom, not only in California but throughout the United States, to give nonphysicians "allied health professional" status. This essentially meant that other mental health professionals could not admit patients/clients to hospitals and were restricted in the types of services they were permitted to render. They had to work under the direction of an attending physician who assumed all medical and legal responsibility for the patient/client along with the clinical decision-making power. In practice, this meant that,

with the exception of psychiatrists, mental health professionals who felt that their patients/clients required hospitalization
would not be able to treat them as long as they remained in
the hospital. The door has been opened for psychologists to
achieve parity in inpatient settings.

There are actually two processes involved in obtaining
hospital privileges: credentialing and privileging. A committee of staff professionals will first review your *credentials* to
ascertain that you fulfill the basic requirements and statutory
regulations to practice. This will include documentation of
your most advanced degree, a copy of your license, copies of
internship and postgraduate residency certificates, and letters
of recommendation from professional peers. You may want
to keep copies of all these on file in the event you decide to
work with more than one hospital. The privileging process
is more complex. It requires the committee to make judgments about particular competencies you have that will qualify you to offer specific types of evaluation (e.g., psychoedu-
cational, projective, personality, neuropsychological assessment) and/or treatment (e.g., hypnosis, biofeedback, family
therapy). The hospital will usually send you a checklist of
services that your profession is permitted to offer. You may
request specific privileges by merely checking those services
you deem yourself qualified to render. You will be asked to
provide documentation of your competency which may
include detailed descriptions of your training, publications,
continuing education certificates, or supervised experiences.
The committee will then rule on your application and inform
you of its decision. Credentialing and privileging decisions
are reviewed annually or biannually. You may petition to
change your privileges. Most hospitals also require your
attendance at medical staff meetings and departmental meetings to maintain your privileged status.

Question 12

What's the best way to market a practice?

Answer

There is not a single best way to market a practice. Since practices differ from one another the same way that individuals are different, it's necessary to understand the uniqueness of your practice to develop a marketing plan. It must also account for the forces that are operating in your local market. The reader is directed to *Fundamentals of Marketing the Private Psychotherapy Practice* (Forman & Forman, 1987) or a basic text devoted to service marketing for a fuller discussion of marketing analysis and planning.

Until recently, many mental health practitioners believed that marketing was unnecessary, and even argued that anyone who marketed their practice was behaving unethically! Today, marketing is a fact of life necessary for survival of a practice.

Although each practice is unique, we'd like to suggest some general guidelines. The foremost recommendation we give is to maintain a marketing orientation. By this, we mean that you need to think of yourself as a provider of services to your community. It is your job to identify the prospective patients/clients who would most benefit from your services, locate your offices where it is most suitable to *them,* have access that is convenient for *them,* and have office hours that meet the needs of these patients/clients. Once these and other elements of your practice, termed *service features,* are in place, you proceed to inform the prospective patients/clients of your availability in ways that are most likely to reach them.

Brochures are among the most widely-used and accepted marketing tools. Probably every practice could benefit from having a brochure for distribution to patients/clients or to referral agents. See Question #45 for a discussion of brochure design. The Division of Psychotherapy and the Division of Independent Practice of the American Psychological Association have produced a variety of very attractive brochures geared toward several specific intervention and target groups. You may call the Administrators (at 1-602-912-5329) for further information.

Making presentations to professional, civic, or parent organizations is also generally accepted as an excellent way of promoting yourself and your practice. Giving speeches is considered ethical because you are providing an educational service. Making presentations is a form of what is known as *personal sales.* If you decide to give talks to community groups, be sure to focus your presentation on the topic at hand. It should not be aimed at promoting your practice or for the direct solicitation of referrals. People can be easily offended by self-aggrandizement, thus damaging your public image. Concentrate on giving the audience what they came to hear.

As regards other general guidelines, it is usually easier to promote a practice rather than an individual. Even if a practice includes just two or three practitioners, the term "center," or "institute," or a practice name can be used. If a practice name implies it is large, it may appear to be a corporate entity and will negatively impact on individuals, referral sources, and Employee Assistance Program professionals. They may choose to interact with individuals rather than risk getting caught in what may seem to be a nameless, faceless bureaucracy. This would not hold true if you are attempting to get managed care contracts. In this case, bigger is usually better because of the economy of scale. Big companies prefer to negotiate with similar organizations. Managed Care Organizations (MCOs) also prefer the ease of multiple specialties so that there is assurance that virtually any type of referral that is made will be handled effectively. This is often the case when provider networks or practices without walls form relationships with MCOs. Also, it is generally easier to promote a specialization than it is to promote a general practice. Of course, this would not hold true in a small town or rural community where there are few other generalists.

Advertising, which refers to paid promotional activities, is not the same as marketing. Whether you should advertise depends on what others in your market are doing. If no one else is advertising in your market, then you probably should not, but use other marketing tools instead. Similarly, yellow pages advertising works in some markets but not in others, although it generally does not work well in bringing in patients/clients at a low cost. Regardless of what marketing approaches you take, you should always document your efforts and their results to determine cost-effectiveness. Marketing efforts can best be monitored by counting responses to particular campaigns. The kind of advertising done by Madison Avenue firms on TV promotes *image*. Historically, this type of advertising is difficult to monitor. Advertising may be subtle or high-pressure. As an example, some ads for high fashion items and fragrances are notorious for leaving the viewer or reader guessing what the ad is trying to sell. Compare that with direct response advertising that implores the viewer or reader to do something immediately. Usually, they implore you to call a toll-free number to place an order. Direct response advertisers can usually tell what form of ad is most effective and how much it costs per inquiry or per order. Certainly this type of ad is better to emulate to get the best value for your advertising dollar.

Finally, never take the advice of an advertising representative. They may know their business, which is selling ads, but they certainly do not know yours. Success, to the advertising representative, is defined as selling advertising space. The more the better. For you, success is defined as number of inquiries to your office, or better still, the number of appointments made as a result of your promotional campaign. Here, the less spent, the better.

Question 13

Is it better to specialize or be a generalist?

Answer

There are several considerations to address here. First, you must enjoy your work. If there is a particular type of disorder or a particular type of patient/client with whom you prefer working, by all means specialize. However, you must be very careful about "painting yourself into a corner." Just as actors may get typecast in their careers and thus miss out on important opportunities for personal and professional success, your colleagues may consider you as a referral resource only in one area. On the other hand, if you are practicing in a highly competitive, professionally saturated area, your specialization in a particular field may help you to stand out from the crowd as a specific specialist on whom other practitioners depend. Specialization is often the critical variable in getting referrals from Employee Assistance Programs (EAPs). You also become the favorite of provider panels, often even if these panels are closed to new providers.

If you make a claim to a specialization, you must be competent in that area. You will need to have specialized training and perhaps certification from a specialty board. This may entail anything from attending continuing education workshops to commitment to formal postgraduate training.

Generally speaking, if you practice in an urban area where the market is highly saturated with a variety of referral problems and specialists, you will almost certainly have to develop a specialty. By contrast, in a relatively unpopulated area, the demands of your caseload will likely require a generalist orientation. In summary, be very careful about how you define your professional skills. This could determine your referral pattern for many years to come.

Question 14

What kind of patients/clients are typically seen in private practice?

Answer

For the past twenty years there have been some radical changes in the types of patients/clients who decide to obtain psychotherapy. In the 1960s and 1970s the typical patient/client was better educated, more verbal, employed in a white collar job, and usually not severely disturbed. Sometimes they were referred to as "the worried well." Patients/clients paid out of their own pockets or health insurance defrayed at least part of the cost of treatment. In addition, they were usually familiar with the psychotherapy process and frequently sought this kind of experience to achieve some personally desired goal(s). In the 1980s and into the 1990s, as the public has become more aware of the benefits of psychotherapy, there has been greater accessibility and acceptance of these services. In today's practice, you are likely to have patients/clients who represent a wide variety of ethnic/cultural backgrounds and lifestyles. A therapist now must educate him/herself about the cultural values of the patients/clients who present for treatment and the orientation toward their use of psychotherapy. For example, you may have to learn to communicate with individuals who may not be accustomed to talking about their problems, or you may have to overcome your discomfort in working with a patient/client for whom avoiding eye contact with you is a sign of respect. Also, some cultural groups may arrive at the office accompanied by several members of their family, and may wish to bring them all into the session. Also, our best advice here is to be sensitive to cultural diversity which dictates what is considered pathological. As an example, a Viet Nam veteran was once treated for Post Traumatic Stress Disorder. He reported how his deceased uncle would visit him in his dreams to counsel him. Was this a hallucination? No, it is common for people of South American heritage to be visited in their dreams.

With the exception of psychiatrists, mental health professionals tend not to see the severely disturbed patient/client in outpatient private practice. This is because the treatment of choice in the current era is medication. Physicians, and in some states nurse practitioners, are the only mental health professionals privileged to dispense psychotropic medications. If you are a nonmedical psychotherapist, you must affiliate with a physician who can monitor the medication of your patients/clients with psychotic and severe mood disorders. Primary care physicians, such as pediatricians and family medicine practitioners, can work closely with you in making decisions about which medications, at what dosage levels, and the patient/client's progress throughout the treatment regimen. Many physicians feel comfortable working with psychotropic medications and actually have developed considerable expertise in using them. Physicians are more likely to cooperate with your treatment plan if they are assured that you are monitoring the patient's response to the medication. Some therapists find it useful to develop a single page physician feedback form that could be mailed or faxed to the physician's office and placed in the patient's chart.

Question 15

What are the advantages of solo versus small group versus large group practices?

Answer

In a solo practice the therapist has complete independence. The freedom to be one's own boss also means that the credit for success does not have to be shared with anyone else. Along with this sense of freedom comes periods of isolation, especially at times when there is a break in the patient/client schedule or when one is in need of collegial consultation. Individual therapists cannot compete with group practices to obtain managed care contracts, while small group practices can provide a sense of security. Emergency coverage can also be shared among group members, thereby reducing stress. Small groups work well until there is interpersonal conflict. Then, difficulties become magnified and the group can become polarized. This can result in an uncomfortable and unproductive work atmosphere. Another difficulty is that when one group member is weak, unproductive, or impaired it will affect the status of the entire group.

Large groups are often very secure because the patient/client flow can almost be guaranteed. There are many opportunities for cross-referrals and contact with colleagues. Because of size it is also possible to contract for services with large organizations. Large practices have an advantage when negotiating with MCOs and can become exclusive providers so that members of the group get virtually all referrals made in their geographic area. In addition, administrative responsibilities can be minimized by clinicians. Unfortunately, there is a price to pay. Large practices are bureaucratic. Administration can be stratified with communication barriers between personnel serving different functions. That may lead to confusion or duplication of effort. For some therapists, the loss of control over fee-setting, availability of office space, or billing can be uncomfortable. Finally, the cost of overhead to the therapists can be quite high, resulting in a reduction in the net hourly rate.

Question 16

How do I decide how much to charge each patient/client?

Answer

In a capitalistic society one may cynically answer: "As much as the traffic will bear!" In reality, there are standards requiring us to take into account the welfare of the consumer. One common standard is the Usual, Customary, and Reasonable (UCR) fee that practitioners in your specialty are charging in the community in which you practice. There is usually a 10 percent to 20 percent range around this figure which takes into consideration years of experience and professional reputation. You can determine prevailing community rates by checking with colleagues or by calling other practitioners' offices and asking how much they charge for procedures such as initial consultation, individual therapy, group therapy, and psychological testing.

Before the advent of managed care, most third-party payers reimbursed at a percentage of the UCR for a given geographic area, commonly set at 50 percent or 80 percent, after the deductible was met. Their definition of customary rate was obtained by examining a sampling of billings submitted by practitioners in the community. Some carriers even constructed a profile of individual practitioners to determine their actual billing rates to establish a payment basis for the following year.

In today's era of managed care, you are paid according to a fee schedule. Third-party payers set specific rates for each type of service. Often the fee schedules are tiered according to level of licensure. When you enter into agreements with HMOs and PPOs, it is a common practice either for rates to be discounted or set at specific dollar amounts. In addition, Medicare, which allowed for independent outpatient billing under Part B for psychologists and social workers, requires that providers agree to accept the established allowable fee currently in effect for their state or in-state region.

As a mental health professional, it is also important to set aside some *pro bono* (i.e., no charge) time; how much is a matter of individual conscience. You may do this by contacting local clergy or public service agencies. Finally, it is important to note that the contemporary consumer of psychotherapeutic services is both sophisticated and sensitive to price. Except for a small number of high income earners, most will shop for the lowest fee. Do not be offended by this, it is a fact of life. Rather, offer the fee that you consider to be reasonable for the type of service and that particular patient/client's financial and psychological circumstances.

Question 17

Should I offer a sliding fee schedule?

Answer

A sliding fee scale is a fee schedule in which the patient/client's earnings and financial circumstances are considered when determining fees. At public facilities these schedules are formal. There are charts to determine fees. In private practice, you have more discretion in determining what your patient/client can reasonably pay. While it is true that your training and professional expertise deserve to be rewarded, your professional obligation is to be available to the community in which you practice. Practitioners in public agencies will appreciate this and demand you will be flexible with referrals.

Note that your reduced rate for services *also* applies to the statement you submit to the third-party payer. You cannot submit a bill at your full UCR when you charged the patient/client less nor can you unilaterally reduce the co-payment. These are considered fraudulent billing practices. As an example, if you decide to reduce your fee from $100 to $50 and the insurance coverage is 50 percent, then you must show a service fee of $50 when submitting the claim. Insurance carriers periodically conduct audits. Your patient/client may be contacted by a carrier's representative and asked about billing and payments. If this information does not correspond with their billing records, you will be asked, at a minimum, to repay them. Carriers can file criminal charges for fraudulent billing practices, report you to your licensing board, and/or make complaints of ethical misconduct to your professional association.

Question 18

Should I accept insurance? If so, what must I know?

Answer

Some practitioners refuse to bill third-party payers. They find it too aggravating and/or too expensive in terms of their overhead. Instead, they ask patients/clients to pay at the time service is rendered and assist the patients/clients in filing claims themselves. As the field becomes increasingly more crowded and competitive, such therapists may find themselves losing patients/clients because other therapists are willing accept co-payments and bill the third-party payer. The *service features* of psychotherapy are important considerations for market position (Forman & Forman, 1987) and often make the difference in whether a patient/client comes to you versus another provider. Patients/clients who simply pay a co-payment of $10 to $25 think they're getting a bargain compared to paying $75 to $100 even when they are reimbursed for the visit by their insurance carrier.

Because of the continuing fluctuations in the economy, employee health benefits are revised almost annually. Through the 1980s we witnessed the erosion of traditional, or indemnity, insurance and the proliferation of managed care organizations (MCOs). In the 1990s we see continued strength of the managed care concept and MCOs are flourishing. We have seen MCOs merging with one another and developing huge corporate structures as these entities struggle to maintain profit levels. Recently, there has been a loosening of the case review process, with easing access to mental health services by beneficiaries and an almost automatic granting of four to six sessions for outpatient visits. The case review process was streamlined, in part, as a cost-saving measure. Outpatient mental health visits show a relatively consistent pattern of being self-limited. More simply, patients/clients tend to leave psychotherapy on their own before their benefits are exhausted. Thus, case managers and mental health MCOs are not usually needed. The vast majority of outpatient patients/clients have a length of stay under eight visits. Only those cases requiring a lengthy course of treatment warrant case management.

In order to stay competitive, it is necessary to be flexible about payment for services. Even though most private practitioners will continue to get paid through a combination of fee-for-service, indemnity plans, and managed care plans, it is worthwhile to become familiar with the following:

a. Freedom of choice legislation in your state
b. Insurance laws in your state
c. What constitutes insurance fraud
d. How to verify benefits and keep track of covered services
e. Types of insurance plans and MCOs in your market
f. How to complete universal (HCFA 1500) claim forms
g. Where to file claims
h. Reimbursement policies on common plans in your market

An excellent resource for anyone in private practice is Richard Small's (1991) *Maximizing Third-Party Reimbursement in your Mental Health Practice.* It is a guide to understanding reimbursement systems as well as the ins and outs of filing claims.

Question 19

What qualities should I seek in associates/partners?

Answer

Most practitioners have little awareness of how essential it is to choose associates or partners wisely. There is nothing that has more potential for business and personal disaster than to choose a partner wrongly. As an example, a close personal friend may not be a good business associate, ruining both your practice and your friendship. If you are considering teaming up with another person, you must respect his/her clinical expertise. After all, your professional reputation is predicated on whom you choose as colleagues. Also, financial and legal liability is directly related to issues of competence. You also need to agree on work styles. If you tend to be organized and bottom line-oriented, you will be unhappy with someone who does not complete paperwork in a timely fashion, or who wants to have a lavish office or more secretarial help. Your personality must also mesh with your partner's traits. Two individuals who need to be the center of attention do not usually work well together. Likewise, an individual who tends to be formal does not work well with someone who dresses casually or calls professionals by their first name. Avoid any whom you consider unethical. In the event one of your partners is accused of wrongdoing, you could be guilty by association. Lawyers can argue that an associate knows either about misconduct, or *should* know, and is therefore negligent and liable. At worst, practicing with an unethical person could become a financial and legal nightmare. At best, it is both disturbing and annoying.

You do not need to have a similar theoretical orientation as your associate. Behavioral and psychodynamic-oriented psychotherapists can work well together in the same practice if each complements the other's professional expertise. It is common in group practices to have a variety of theoretical orientations and skills so as to provide an array of psychological services.

We would urge anyone who is considering taking on an associate or partner to have a trial period. Begin by sharing space and then increasingly share responsibilities. You can liken it to an engagement before marriage. After an extended period of time, perhaps a year or more, you may then consider a partnership arrangement. To assure each partner's best interests, each should retain his/her own attorney. All agreements should be put in writing. In this way, all parties can be protected against liability problems.

An area that is often missed when partnerships are formed is life insurance. A type of policy, known as *First to Die*, allows the surviving partner(s) to receive compensation so that the practice can continue in the event of a partner's demise. There are other types of insurance available which can provide for practice continuation and can be matched to your particular situation and needs. This is a subject that should be addressed with a life insurance or financial planning professional.

Question 20

What is the status of prescription privileges?

Answer

Most mental health professionals do not realize there are already several nonphysician professions that have obtained limited prescription privileging including optometry, podiatry, dentistry, and nursing. Currently, the profession of psychology is pursuing several avenues of entry into medication prescribing privileges. Psychologists have already practiced these privileges in the Indian Health Service and in the Veteran's Administration Hospital facilities. The Prescribing Psychologist's Register (1-305-931-3552 or ppr@aol.com) has been conducting workshops for psychologists around the country. They offer an extensive curriculum over a series of seven courses.

There continues to be much controversy in the profession of psychology regarding prescription privileges. Surveys indicate that psychologists are still divided on this issue, although the trend is toward greater support of prescription privileges particularly by the leadership of psychologist organizations. The American Psychological Association has formally supported this initiative. If pharmaceutical manufacturers are correct, prescription privileges will be obtained in the not too distant future. They are already sponsoring workshops for psychologists at national conventions, perceiving them as a potential source of new business.

The American Psychological Association's Division of Psychopharmacology has established guidelines for training in psychopharmacology, as has the Division of Clinical Psychology. The U.S. Department of Defense also established a training curriculum for psychologists. There is also considerable activity in the legislative arena. See DeLeon, Fox and Graham (1991) for an excellent discussion of the major issues surrounding prescription privileges for psychologists.

Question 21

What are the most common malpractice threats faced by practitioners? Should I be worried?

Answer

Kenneth Pope (1989) reported on malpractice complaint and claims data collected by the American Psychological Association Insurance Trust between 1976 and 1988. The major complaint made against psychologists concerned sexual improprieties with patients/clients. Just over 20 percent of all complaints fell into this category, but it accounted for over 53 percent of the costs associated with settling *all* malpractice claims.

The second most frequent cause for filing a malpractice complaint was incorrect treatment (i.e., incompetence), accounting for just over 13 percent of all claims filed. Material loss attributed to professional evaluation made up 8.5 percent of claims, while breach of confidentiality made up 6.4 percent. Only 6 percent of the complaints were due to a violation of ethical, legal, or professional standards in billing practices or fee collection efforts. Violation of the *duty to warn* standard was implicated in less than one-half of one percent of all claims.

As long as psychotherapists do not become sexually

involved with current or former patients/clients, practice competently within their specialty, and otherwise follow the ethical and professional standards of their discipline, there is little risk in having a malpractice suit filed against them. However, it is much easier to become involved in complaints to licensing boards and professional associations—even if the grievance is frivolous. All complaints are treated as valid until evidence to the contrary is established. For psychologists, who are members of the American Psychological Association, and obtained their insurance from the American Psychological Association Insurance Trust, the Trust is a valuable resource. They maintain a toll-free number to assist you in complaints filed against you (1-800-477-1200).

Question 22

What are the implications of managed care for private practitioners?

Answer

In the beginning of the 1990s, managed care had become more available to the consumer than traditional indemnity health coverage. In indemnity plans, the insured goes to a licensed provider who is reimbursed a dollar amount or fixed percentage of the fee charged. The insured is responsible for paying the rest of the fee. As health care costs rose at rates much faster than inflation, indemnity plans became much more expensive for businesses offering health insurance to their employees. Businesses were concerned because the costs of providing health insurance, as part of the employee benefit packages, were eroding profits. The first way of managing health care costs was to modify the benefit design: increase deductibles and co-insurance payments, decrease annual maximums, and place caps on lifetime maximum payments for certain services. Other business people developed what are now called Preferred Provider Organizations (PPOs) or provider networks. In this arrangement, an entity is established which serves as a broker between a group of providers and groups of consumers. In essence, the company establishes a set of policies for providers and asks them to agree to see their insureds for a fixed fee. This negotiated fee is routinely lower than prevailing usual, customary, and reasonable fees (UCRs). The provider is asked to accept this reduced fee in exchange for quick payment, guaranteed referrals, exclusive listing, or some other inducement. In actual practice today, the only inducement for a practitioner to join a network is to have access to a cohort of insureds that would otherwise be unavailable. The organization then promotes their plan to employers claiming that it can reduce costs while maintaining quality services. There are literally dozens of PPOs in existence, each operating with similar principles but subtly different from one another. It is often said in health insurance circles "If you've seen one PPO, you've seen one PPO."

Health Maintenance Organizations (HMOs) were established by federal legislation in 1973. They are similar to PPOs in that cost containment was factored into their ideological roots. However, as a brainchild of the Nixon administration, the original idea was that not only would healthcare costs be contained, but that employers would realize cost savings. Costs would be shifted to the consumers who chose to get their healthcare elsewhere, or to obtain more services than they could receive under the plan. The major way that an HMO differs from a PPO is that in the former providers are typically salaried employees, sometimes known as "docs in a box!" This is less so for mental health providers, who may be in private practice, but contracted to provide services to HMO members in much the same way as PPO subscribers. The differences which may exist could be in benefit limits, case management requirements, or rates paid to providers.

In recent years, there has been the growth of organizations that contract for the behavioral health component of health care. In this situation, many different MCOs contract with specialty mental health plans which perform referral and case management functions. Over 50 percent of the 150 million Americans enrolled in managed care plans have their mental health services handled by one of three large firms: Magellan Health Services, Value Behavioral Health, or Merit Behavioral Care (Anon., 1997).

One advantage to providers who participate in managed care plans may include guaranteed referrals. Some plans require their subscribers to obtain a referral from their primary care physicians or plan administrators, while others have subscribers select from a list of providers that is supplied to them. Many plans limit the number and/or types of providers within regions, so a provider could receive considerable referrals if the plan covers many people. It is not uncommon for plans to have streamlined procedures for filing claims and have provisions for rapid processing so that payment is guaranteed quickly. For the provider, this could translate to a reduction in administrative overhead associated with running a practice, which offsets the lower fee received.

On the down side, there is not always a guarantee of referrals. If a plan covers relatively few lives, it could present an inconvenience. The provider may have to spend time following a variety of complex administrative procedures for just a few patients/clients. Another problem is the level of reimbursement. The provider may receive half or even less than his/her UCR. This requires the provider to work twice as many hours to earn the same amount of money that could be earned outside of network. Another problem is that case management procedures can also be cumbersome and interfere with the clinical management of patients/clients. Finally, the treatment philosophy of the provider may clash with that held by the MCO. One of the authors once worked with an MCO that was fanatically dedicated to short-term interventions. Six sessions were approved for a patient. During the sixth session the patient reported experiencing homicidal fantasies about his ex-wife. The MCO approved just one more session to resolve this issue!

Question 23

How is reimbursement influencing clinical decision making?

Answer

Constraints on psychotherapeutic interventions by managed care pose the greatest threat to quality of care. They include limiting authorization for hospitalization, limiting sessions of outpatient psychotherapy, and refusal to pay for psychological testing. While these constraints effectively contain mental health care costs, time consuming preauthorization procedures for obtaining emergency hospitalization are potentially dangerous for your patients/clients, particularly if suicide is an issue. Many hospitals simply will not accept patients irrespective of their condition if third-party payers have not authorized reimbursement prior to admission. As to time-limiting psychotherapy, short-term therapy has proven to be successful in many instances, but there are a variety of conditions that require longer-term treatment (e.g., schizophrenia, personality disorders, adult survivors of incest). Premature termination in these cases can cause more harm than no psychotherapy at all. A frequent practice of managed care plans is to exclude coverage for psychological assessment. This is penny-wise and dollar-foolish since a thorough diagnostic evaluation can be essential in determining both length and type of treatment. As an example, one of the authors had a case in which an adolescent male was failing in school. He had a long history of underachievement, but not as severe as he presented at the initial visit. Diagnostically, the question to be addressed was concerned with determining whether this is a clinically significant depression? Could there be a specific learning disability? Or maybe there is borderline intelligence. The MCO refused to pay for the administration of the WAIS-R as medically unnecessary.

Although you may not be reimbursed by a plan, once you initiate work with patients/clients it is unethical to terminate treatment or provide inadequate service. You may be liable if you do so, even if the HMO or PPO refuses to pay you. Therefore, it is incumbent upon you to understand the nature of your responsibilities when you decide to accept managed care patients/clients in your practice.

MCOs often establish criteria for treatment continuation which is related to diagnosis, level of functioning, and/or goal attainment. Clinicians are often limited to establishing a couple of goals that must be achieved within a short period of time. Even if there are more significant problems, or ones that cannot be placed in simple behavioral terms, clinicians must still assist patients/clients with attainable goals. This has created frustration for many therapists who, due to imposed time constraints, feel they cannot provide the best therapy for their patients/clients.

Question 24

What is the average number of outpatient therapy visits? How many are reimbursable?

Answer

Expectations of psychotherapists about the duration of treatment are at odds with the actual length of treatment obtained by patients/clients. Lowry and Ross (1997) surveyed 1000 experienced psychologists in private practice regarding their views of how many sessions are required to restore optimal functioning to an individual. It was generally agreed that 30-40 sessions are needed for successfully treating problems routinely encountered in private outpatient psychotherapy practice. Problems related to work or adjustment were thought to require 11 to 20 sessions, while more significant disorders needed a longer course of treatment.

Studies done by Lakin Phillips (1987) have identified a national average of six sessions for individual outpatient psychotherapy. He contacted the authors of published studies and reevaluated their findings in terms of percent of patients/clients remaining in treatment following each session. He found that across populations a negatively accelerating (decay) curve existed. Therapists' theoretical orientation did not have any effect. Using the same method of computation employed by Phillips, Forman (1990) reported that the mean number of sessions for families was three and for couples it was two sessions, at a university-based outpatient clinic. Apparently the number of sessions actually attended by patients/clients differs dramatically from the duration of treatment needed to achieve the most favorable results. We would agree with Lowry and Ross's (1997) contention that psychotherapy is underutilized by patients/clients.

Each therapist has his/her own standards for what is an acceptable number of sessions for a given condition. Some have found that by educating patients/clients at the beginning of treatment as to the nature of therapy and its length results in diminished attrition. If a patient/client agrees to come in and work on a problem for eight sessions with the possibility of reviewing progress and contracting for additional sessions at that point, she/he will likely honor the commitment.

The number of sessions allowed by insurance carriers appears to defy the laws of logic. Some companies allow one visit per seven-day period. Some allow 20 visits per year (as specified in the federal HMO Act), and still others do not specify a number of visits, but instead state an annual dollar limit. When beginning treatment with a patient/client, you must call the carrier to verify benefits. Many practitioners have prepared forms that include questions such as: What is the annual maximum for inpatient and outpatient benefits? Is psychological testing included in the annual maximum? Is session reimbursement at a fixed rate, or percentage of UCR? Is there a co-payment required, and if so, how much? What are the exclusions (e.g., certain diagnoses? DSM-IV V codes)? What are the limitations for preexisting conditions or prior psychological treatment? How much is the deductible? How much of the deductible has already been met? What services are covered? (e.g., individual therapy, group therapy, family therapy, hypnosis, psychological testing), are the services of licensed psychologists, mental health therapists, social workers, marriage and family therapists covered? What are the requirements for obtaining authorization for initial treatment and for additional visits? Is a referral from the primary care physician required? Are HCFA 1500 claim forms accepted or are special claim forms required? To what address should bills be sent?

Question 25

How do I find out which managed care organizations are operating in my community and how do I join them?

Answer

Your patients/clients will inform you of the managed care plans in your community. Unfortunately, many of them may be closed to new providers. Also, other providers can also inform you. Still another source is the billing department of a physician's office. Often they will gladly provide names, addresses, and phone numbers of the provider relations representatives of the plans with which they most often work. Finally, there are commercially available lists that are advertised in professional association publications, such as the *APA Monitor*.

Whether or not you join a particular MCO depends on the kind of practice you have and your willingness to tolerate lower fees and red tape. Failure to participate in managed care can mean loss of substantial referrals in some markets. But, since no one can predict what the field will be like in the future, the situation could change within the next few years. Some observers of trends in business suggest that business cycles generally last approximately seven years. Trends for various professions seem to run a similar course. It also appears that when there is plenty of work and good money to be made there is massive entry into that field. Subsequently, the field becomes crowded, competition increases, individual income or salaries drop, and there is an exodus by practitioners. The cycle repeats itself and those who remain in the field eventually succeed, simply because of persistence. We don't know if this will hold true for psychotherapists, but we remain optimistic.

If you want to join an MCO panel, start by contacting the provider relations office and request an application. If the panel is not currently open to your discipline you may be told to wait. After completing the application it undergoes a credential review. If you are turned down for any reason there may be an internal appeal process. Otherwise you are out of luck. However, if you find out about a plan that is relatively new you may have a ground floor opportunity. With the large behavioral health management firms that provide mental health referral and case management for many plans, once you are on a couple of panels you may find that you are automatically placed on others. There have been many occasions when we were contacted by someone requesting treatment and who found our names in a provider directory from a carrier we did not know existed.

Many psychotherapists are not positively inclined toward managed care. Some consider it unethical to work with them in any way. Nick Cummings, Ph.D., a psychologist who founded a national psychological services managed care entity and former APA president, suggested guidelines for evaluating MCOs. In a presentation at the American Psychological Association's Annual Convention, he listed ten ways to identify mismanaged care (1991), and recommended avoiding those organizations which are guilty of the following:

1. Participation in the network is open to all who apply. This indicates that management is more interested in quantity than quality.

2. A fee is charged for joining, suggesting that the company is undercapitalized and may not even have any contracts. They use membership or application fees for operating or marketing costs.

3. Nonpractitioners are used as case managers, making case management a clerical, rather than clinical issue.

4. There are barriers to accessing mental health services. Poor quality plans do not allow patients/clients to self-refer. Instead, they may be forced to go through a primary care physician or maze of paperwork before getting an appointment with a psychotherapist as much as two weeks later.

5. There is a focus on cost containment, not clinical efficiency. In practice session limits, deductibles, and co-payments can discourage utilization of mental health services and these serve as artificial means of keeping costs down.

6. The plan benefits for mental health services are narrowly defined. For example, only crisis intervention is a covered benefit, or certain diagnostic categories are excluded, such as marital or parent-child problems.

7. Leadership is overly concerned with business or medical decision-making. In such entities, managers are exclusively holders of MBA or MD degrees. Business concerns or medical establishment pressures will override clinical issues.

8. There are no provisions for training or continuing education. Quality firms assist their providers in working with their managed care system and provide support for learning efficient treatment strategies.

9. Quality assurance is ignored. A quality company must be concerned about the overall quality of care that is provided through its network. Although formal quality assurance procedures in managed care organizations is unusual now, it will become increasingly more important in the future.

10. There is no commitment to research. A well-managed plan seeks to improve its services to subscribers by ongoing data-based research to determine the effectiveness of interventions.

Other concerns that practitioners often have about MCOs are pragmatic. There are three primary concerns raised most often: Will I get referrals? How much will I get paid and when, and how much paperwork and time on the phone will be involved? The best way to find out is to address these concerns with plan administrators and with colleagues who are already on the network. In our experience, there are no MCOs that will completely satisfy every practitioner. You should evaluate any plan in accordance with your own needs and willingness to abide by the procedures. A good point to remember is that if you join a network, then later decide it's not right for you, you can resign.

Question 26

Is it better to develop exclusive relationships with MDs and/or lawyers or to practice independently?

Answer

As with most things in life, it is not usually wise to put all your eggs in one basket. You leave yourself open to undue influences on your clinical and personal decisions if you must rely on one person for a living. The greater the variety of your referral relationships, the richer and more successful will be your practice. Does this mean you should avoid cultivating some close and mutually beneficial referral sources?

No, there are usually several referral sources that will provide the bulk of patients/clients that are directly referred to you. You must continually express your appreciation. This may include thank you notes, monthly summaries of progress, or telephone conferences.

In today's marketplace, referral is a primary function of what provider lists you are on as opposed to your experience or clinical excellence. Thus, it is doubly important to have others notice you. Otherwise, you are but one more name on a provider list. Attorney referrals are the one important source independent of the above considerations. They are not faced with the same limitations of selecting from MCO provider lists.

Question 27

How do I develop a practice if I relocate to a new community?

Answer

Regardless of the motivation for your move, it will ease the transition if you contact the professional associations and regional organizations in the new community for relevant information about current professional practice and apply for membership. You must also obtain an application for licensure, and, if need be, begin studying for any examinations you may be required to take. You may also want to find out if there are any networks of mental health professionals that meet on a regular basis. If you have acquaintances in your old community who know practitioners in the new one, get their names and call on them when you come to town. You can also begin to identify sites in which you may be able to begin practicing. You may want to consider joining a group practice as a means of having a professional support system to help in getting established. Basically, the rules for developing a practice in a new location are the same as developing a practice in the old location.

Question 28

How long does it take to get paid from patients? Third party payers?

Answer

Many providers collect the patient/client fee or co-payment at the end of each session. In this way, you do not run the risk of building a huge, and sometimes uncollectible balance. A pay-as-you-go policy is also useful in avoiding the ill feelings that can breed in a debtor-lender relationship. Paying at the end of each session also reduces the overhead necessitated by billing and record-keeping costs. Billing accounts for 5-15 percent of practice overhead. Nevertheless, some practitioners prefer to bill their patients/clients on a monthly basis. It is reasonable to expect payment within thirty days of billing. Regardless of which method you choose, you should have a written financial policy governing all patients/clients. They should read and sign a statement attesting to their understanding of the payment policy. It should include your expectations of when they should pay and the consequences of late payments. Many professionals charge interest on overdue payments.

If your patient/client does not make payments when expected it might be necessary to initiate reminder notices, along with a copy of your financial policy statement. If this is not effective, you may have to turn the account over to a collection agency. If you decide to pursue collection procedures, expect to be charged between one-third and half of your outstanding balance. Some therapists guard against these charges by including a statement in their financial responsibility form that holds the patient/client responsible for all fees required to collect unpaid balances. The best way to avoid the aggravation of problem collections is to insist on prompt payment.

Third-party payers typically take from four to six weeks from the time of billing to reimburse you. Some states have enacted laws that stipulate the timely payments from insurance carriers. For example, Florida Statute # 627.613 states "The insurer will pay monthly all benefits then due." Some practitioners in Florida have found it helpful to place a sticker on each claim noting this. Additionally, many providers place a status call to the carrier after 60 or 90 days. This is to ascertain what is holding up payment of the claim. This information may be useful in getting the process moving. The most common responses to status calls are that the claim form was never received, a reply to an inquiry was lost, the claim is pending review, the patient/client has no mental health benefits in spite of what is stated in the patient/client's benefit handbook, the computer system is down, the claim was paid months ago, a check was sent to an incorrect address, and the only claims representative who is capable of handling your inquiry is on maternity leave for three more months. We are not making up these excuses. They are actual responses we have received.

Yet, no matter what you do, it could still take a considerable length of time to be paid on a claim. The personal record of one of the authors is two years and nine months.

However, with the aid of electronic claims submissions, turn-around time can be more rapid. For instance, in Florida, electronically submitted claims to Medicare are routinely paid within three weeks. They will even deposit the money directly into your bank account.

Question 29

When and how can I refuse to see a patient/client?

Answer

At first contact, you have the right to decline or refuse to accept any patient/client. Once you accept a patient/client for treatment, you must have a valid reason for terminating them. You have the right to expect certain responsibilities from your patients/clients. We recommend that you present to them a written agreement to study that indicates responsibilities to you and to the treatment process. As an example, we require notifications of at least 24 hours for appointment cancellation. If this does not occur, the patient/client is responsible for paying for the appointment.

Note that you cannot refuse to continue to see a patient/client for economic reasons. This is called "abandonment" and is contrary to mental health professional ethics, as well as grounds for a lawsuit. If a referred individual on an initial visit cannot afford your fees or has a need for services you cannot offer, you still have a responsibility to recommend another source of help.

Once you have accepted a patient/client, you may refuse to continue treatment for the following reasons: (a) failure to comply with your treatment regimen, (b) you are not competent to treat their problems, (c) the patient/client will see you only at times that are unreasonable, (d) the patient/client comes to sessions under the influence of drugs or alcohol, or (e) you are experiencing unabated counter-transference. If for any of these reasons you terminate a patient/client, it is your responsibility to give the patient/client the reason(s) for termination, offer treatment alternatives, and to document this in the patient/client's chart.

Question 30

What should I do with a subpoena regarding a patient/client?

Answer

At some point in your career, you will be subpoenaed in connection with legal matters regarding a patient/client. You will be asked to provide information regarding your patient/client, and you may be asked to have a deposition taken of your expert opinion. You are entitled to charge a fee for the expenses incurred in collecting and mailing information required by the court. You are also entitled to charge a fee for your professional opinion. Most professionals charge their usual hourly rate plus preparation and travel time. Insist on being paid in advance of the deposition. Often, when you are served a subpoena to appear at a hearing or deposition, it will be accompanied by a small check (e.g., $5-$10). When you are offered such a modest fee simply contact the attorney's office who requested your appearance and inform him/her of your fee.

You can refuse to appear at a deposition or subsequent court hearing if you are not adequately compensated. In the event you are asked to provide testimony, insist you do so in the capacity of an expert. If you are a *fact witness*, only testifying about what you observed, you may not be entitled to be paid for your testimony (Woody, 1991).

Any time that you are served with a subpoena you should contact the patient/client's attorney to protect the patient/client's confidentiality. The attorney may decide that the order of the court is inappropriate. In this case, he/she has the right to appeal before supplying requested information. Sometimes, we have received subpoenas written by a lawyer that is not court-ordered. One should obtain legal counsel to determine the appropriate course of action.

Question 31

How do I keep abreast of advances in the field?

Answer

There are a myriad of journals and newsletters available to mental health practitioners. These can be obtained by going to your local university library or by contacting your national and state professional organization. There are ever-increasing opportunities for continuing education courses and seminars. Most states now require evidence of continuing education credits, which is required for renewal of professional licenses. Many professional journals are now offering CEU's if you read their articles, then submit and pass a written test.

You may also seek out senior colleagues as supervisors or consultants, particularly in difficult or unusual cases.   In some locales, therapists form peer supervision groups for professional advice and for support and encouragement. You will find that interacting with colleagues around interesting professional issues and new techniques is a stimulating and growth enhancing experience.   It also prevents professional burnout.   The biggest challenge facing practitioners is not *how* to keep up with the field, but rather how to *select* the topics that are most relevant to your current practice.

Question 32

How do I avoid burnout?

Answer

Burnout is common among mental health professionals who have high expectations for themselves and their patients/clients, but face obstacles to achieving their goals. Professionals experience it as they would chronic depression. The signs of burnout include irritability, tension, short-temperedness, working too hard, losing interest in customary social activities, thinking about leaving the industry, becoming perseverative in your thought process, deluding yourself about your abilities or energy level, and a general sense of malaise.

Treatment or prevention of burnout includes learning to relax, setting limits on your work, and enforcing these limits. Periodic diversions like hobbies or weekend excursions get you away from routine and stressors.   They can give you a renewed interest in your work.

Some practitioners find that regularly scheduled peer supervision groups helps to decrease the feelings of isolation. A second benefit is that participants can focus on difficult cases, thereby reducing tunnel vision in their clinical work. Other therapists find that teaching can provide the kind of stimulation they need to remain fresh in their professional practice. Finally, many therapists focus on physical fitness, exercise, good nutritional habits, and adequate sleep. This prevents buildup of stress and increases energy.

Question 33

How do I best manage my professional and personal time?

Answer

Each of us works at our own pace. The best general advice we can offer is to avoid putting pressure on yourself. You may be the kind of individual who thrives on challenges, the classic therapist personality. Not having a full schedule may be stressful to you. Others may not want to work weekends or evening hours. Thus, some therapists put in 50 to 60 hours a week, loving every minute of it. Others set 25 hour limits over the course of a week, or limit the number of hours per day that they are willing to work. What is important is that you match your personal and professional goals to your work schedule. Stick to the limits you have set for yourself.

Question 34

How important is it for non-MDs to be board certified?

Answer

In medicine, it is expected that specialists will be board certified, or at least board-eligible, in their fields. Eligibility for board certification requires completion of an approved residency or fellowship in a particular specialization. For example, certification in Internal Medicine requires completion of a medicine residency. The internist can further specialize, in say cardiology or gastroenterology by completing a fellowship in that specialty that then leads to board eligibility. Board certification or eligibility thus means that the physician has successfully completed a designated training curriculum and has been exposed to a specified body of knowledge.

For non-MDs outside of academic settings, certification by a specialty board does not necessarily lead to recognition or additional financial compensation. Also, there is no uniformity across boards and no established standards or curricula. Consequently, most patients/clients do not know what it means for a mental health professional to be board certified. Some physicians may desire that people they refer to have board certification because of their own professional socialization. However, the major reason physicians have for referring their patients is based on the reputation of the clinician or whether they are on a particular MCO provider list. Likewise, third-party payers do not place any distinction upon board certification for referrals or fees. One of the authors had a conversation with an MCO executive. He had no interest in considering board certification for admission to their provider panel.

You may therefore consider board certification irrelevant to your professional goals. However, in today's competitive market any distinction between you and your peers to enhance your position may result in more referrals. The past decade has witnessed a proliferation of new certifying boards. Many have grandparenting periods. That is, your years of experience alone qualify you for admission. The fact that certification has become more popular speaks to a growing need for psychotherapists to develop specializations.

Another trend in the practice of psychology is that the American Psychological Association (APA) is developing a nosology for professional practice. The APA has appointed a commission called Commission for the Recognition of Specialties and Proficiencies in Professional Psychology (CRSPPP). Currently, CRSPPP has a thorough set of guidelines that are used to decide what is to be called a specialty. Several specialties and/or proficiencies have already been submitted to CRSPPP including Disability Determination and Management, Emergency and Trauma Psychology, and Serious Mental Illness. The specialty of Health Psychology has been formally recognized already.

Criticisms of this process are similar to those leveled at board certification. Recognition is not linked to the marketplace.

Question 35

How can I reduce hassles with insurance carriers? What can I do if claims are denied, withheld, late, or reimbursed incompletely?

Answer

One of the best ways to work with third-party pay sources is through prevention. First, verify benefits for new patients/clients *prior* to their initial consultation with you. Patients/clients are notoriously poor students of their health benefits. They may make appointments with you honestly believing they have substantial benefits where none exist. When you do verify, ask to whom you are speaking and make a note of it in your file. Employers often give erroneous information. Identifying them may save you a lot of money. Some providers use insurance worksheets and include one in every new patient/client file. If you know in advance what coverage is available you should not be surprised when you receive the explanation of benefits accompanying, or in lieu of, payment from the carrier. We can not underestimate the importance of accurate, detailed, and complete paperwork when submitting claims. We have had claims denied for the following missing information: no birthdate, no diagnosis, incorrect procedure code, no social security number, and no proof that a 20-year-old dependent was a student.

Understanding and complying with the payer's rules and procedures was less important prior to the spread of MCOs. Now, it is essential to know the rules for reimbursement for each patient/client's carrier. Being denied payment for a claim because the case manager authorized fewer visits than you thought you needed is not uncommon. For each MCO contract you sign, be certain you understand and follow the rules. If you are not paid because you made an error in following the procedures for documentation or obtaining approvals you can not hold the patient/client responsible for paying a fee.

Another aspect of collections that is important for you is to know the laws governing insurance payments in your state. You are then in a position to put pressure on the carrier if they violate the statute. One of the actions you can take is to contact your state insurance commission or regulatory office. They are responsive to complaints from dissatisfied consumers and providers because next year's budget allocations may be based on the volume of complaints they received. Some, but not all, carriers are responsive to insurance commission queries. You may get action by simply noting on the bottom of correspondence you send to the carrier that a copy is being simultaneously sent to the state insurance commission.

It is very important that you document everything you do in connection with getting payment of claim. You should note names, dates, and content of conversations with everyone with whom you had a telephone conversation within the claims administrator's office. These notes should be written in the patient/client's file.

A copy of any correspondence to the carrier should also be sent to the state insurance commission. If you do not get satisfaction within a reasonable time frame do not hesitate to file a formal complaint. The Consumer Affairs Bureau Chief for the Florida Department of Insurance told us that his office is deluged with complaints about insurance carriers. He went on to say that he appreciates being contacted by providers who see patterns of offenses by particular carriers. In this way, his office is aided in narrowing down which companies to investigate. It is probably similar in other states, so if you have repeated problems with a carrier, make an official complaint, with complete documentation of the difficulty.

Sometimes it is effective to call and try to resolve your concern over the phone. A handy phrase to use is "May I speak with your supervisor, please?" if you do not get immediate results. It may be necessary to bring your concerns to the next level and send written justification to the carrier if a claim is denied and you feel it was unwarranted on clinical grounds. One of the authors had the experience of having a claim for inpatient family therapy denied for an adolescent. A letter arguing that family therapy is an accepted form of treatment which is beneficial to the patient and may ultimately reduce costs to the carrier for continuing mental health care, resulted in payment of the claim. Similarly, a case manager declined an approval for couple therapy. After a letter was sent explaining how the patient had a diagnosable mood disorder and documented initial improvement of her condition, approval was granted.

As an aside, if you have concerns about dealing with MCOs your complaints to state insurance regulatory bodies may fall on deaf ears. HMOs are not insurance companies at all. HMOs are health service delivery contractors. Health care services are delivered to subscribers on a *contract* basis and are governed by those laws dealing with contracts. PPOs are intermediaries between beneficiaries and the insurance carriers. They serve as *third party administrators* and technically are outside of the rules that apply to the carriers, although they may be responsive to inquiries by the insurance regulators.

Since HMOs and PPOs are not governed by insurance laws, and if you are having difficulties with collection, you have more limited options available. If you feel compelled to complain to your state's consumer affairs office or local state or district attorney, notifying the MCO about your intentions may bring about a speedy resolution.

Question 36

What are the legal and tax requirements for working as an independent contractor versus being an employee?

Answer

Many group practices have associates who are independent contractors rather than salaried employees. Some therapists who have had what they believed was contractor status found out otherwise when the government stepped in. To be considered an independent contractor a clinician must have total authority for clinical management of their patients/clients and how they practice. That is, he/she directs what, when, and how the work should be performed. Additionally, the independent contractor should project an image to the public of an independent practitioner. Independent contractors, have the right to hire and supervise their own employees to perform specific tasks such as psychological testing, and can establish the rate of pay for their employees. According to the law, independent contractors must also have written contracts delineating them as such. The contract must stipulate manner and amount of payment, regulations governing both parties, and why and how the contract can be terminated. Contractors are self-employed. As such, they must have appropriate licensure and liability insurance to practice independently. For income tax purposes, they receive 1099 forms rather than W-2 forms. As self-employed persons, taxes on earnings must be filed quarterly. Under the United States Tax Code, taxes on earnings are due immediately. The IRS allows you until the end of each quarter to file and pay them.

Question 37

Should I choose to be an independent contractor instead of being an employee?

Answer

Over the past few years, the IRS tightened the definition of who is an employee in many fields, including mental health. So, the choice may not be yours to make. If you are treated as an independent contractor for the convenience of the employer, it may be disallowed later with tax consequences for both parties. For example, if a practitioner appoints a part-time therapist as an independent contractor who is not yet licensed, the arrangement is not truly a contractor relationship. The unlicensed therapist must be paid as a W-2 employee until her/his license is obtained and a contract prepared. The advantage to the employee is that she/he has limited liability and may be eligible for whatever benefits are paid to other employees. The down side is that a variety of tax deductions that are available to people who are self-employed cannot be taken.

There are several advantages to being self-employed, not the least of which is the sense of being one's own boss and the freedom that goes with it. There are numerous tax advantages to having one's own business. These include deductions for malpractice insurance, license renewal fees, continuing education expenses, vehicle used in the course of business, and more. One of the best features is the retirement investing that is available for self-employed persons, which has a much higher dollar limit than Individual Retirement Accounts (IRAs). There is also a way of deducting 100 percent of family medical expenses that is only available to people who have their own businesses and are married. (This is contained in Section 105 of the IRS Tax Code.) Unfortunately, self-employed people, even those who have a sole proprietorship (i.e., solo practice) are subject to self-employment tax instead of paying FICA. For those who are at the 28 percent tax bracket, the addition of self-employment tax can mean they are being taxed at a rate of over 40 percent! Of course, this tax is on what is left *after* deducting the cost of doing business and related expenses. You can obtain information and forms from the IRS by calling 1-800-829-1040.

Question 38

What are the legal consequences of signing off for unlicensed or nonreimbursable therapists on insurance claims?

Answer

"Signing off," or signing insurance claim forms for services that were rendered by someone else, is a widespread practice. It is fraudulent if the actual provider of the service is not identified. Many carriers will reimburse for services that are provided by someone under the supervision of a licensed provider who is otherwise eligible for reimbursement.

There have been cases in which the insurance company learned fraud had been committed. In a well-publicized Kentucky case, in addition to requiring the offending provider to pay back the money that was obtained by fraudulent means, the carrier filed a criminal complaint against the provider, who was later convicted and sent to prison. It is noteworthy that the therapist, a social worker, was accused of committing fraud, but the psychiatrist, who signed off and was equally guilty, was not prosecuted. In spite of cases like this one, signing off remains a common practice. Possibly because it is considered trivial by some, possibly because they think they can get away with it.

The definition of what constitutes supervision has been radically changed over the past several years. In essence, the supervisor must be on-site during the time of service. There have been several major lawsuits brought against medical teaching hospitals for failing to comply with this definition.

Question 39

How much is typical of overhead for an office?

Answer

First, let us define overhead. It includes the following items: rent, furniture, utilities, answering service, salaries, pager, postage, office machines and equipment, office supplies, psychological testing supplies, accounting services, billing expenses (e.g., supply of HCFA 1500 forms, special software for electronic billing, billing service) transportation, continuing professional education, professional memberships, subscriptions, business insurance, malpractice insurance, license renewal fees, phones, janitorial/cleaning, and marketing.

Some practitioners can operate without some amenities or have figured out ways to keep some fixed costs very low.

The range for total overhead runs between 20 percent and 40 percent of gross practice revenues. The average expenditure for most practitioners we have talked with is 25-30 percent. This is consistent with results of a national survey which reported overhead accounts for approximately 25 percent of gross practice revenue (Anon., 1997).

There is currently strong debate as to whether to have support staff or to self-bill, handle collections, and make appointments. This depends upon whether the majority of your practice is self-paying or comes from third-party payers. It has become increasingly more complex to obtain authorization for various treatment modalities and to keep up with treatment plans. If you are willing to spend *hours* on the clerical aspects and paperwork needed to ensure payment, then your need for support staff is minimal. If, on the other hand, you are unwilling to exert the time and effort necessary to negotiate the mental health payment bureaucracies, then you should pay someone to do it for you.

Another major concern that practitioners fail to consider is the cost associated with not having a person to speak with callers when the therapist is unavailable. Many potential patients are tentative about scheduling an initial appointment. An encouraging person will increase the probability of attendance. An answering machine message might result in the loss of that patient/client. Also, when patients/clients call to cancel their appointments a person can remind them of their responsibilities or can reschedule the appointment. Since this happens so frequently, the practitioner can potentially save thousands of dollars in lost revenue by having a person answer the telephone.

Question 40

What do I need to know about Employee Assistance Programs (EAPs)?

Answer

As we advise our colleagues: when working with referral sources, ask not what they can do for you, but ask what you can do for them. When working with EAP professionals it is essential to understand both the needs of the patient/client *and* the needs of the employer. What may appear to be a humane organization providing its workers with a means of getting help for emotional difficulties is also a company that must make profits to ensure its survival. Informed management understands that it is more cost-effective to assist troubled employees than to replace them. Larger companies must also comply with the Americans with Disabilities Act which compels corporations to assist their employees. Whatever the motivation, no company wants to be burdened with open-ended psychotherapeutic services of indeterminate length. Rather, they are interested in contracting with providers who share the goal of returning the employee to work as soon as possible. EAP professionals appreciate a therapist who is oriented toward providing solutions to problems affecting job performance.

Michael Wakefield, EAP manager for one of the largest EAPs in the U.S., states that EAP professionals generally appreciate a therapist who works in an atmosphere of mutual trust and respect. Often therapists assume that they are the only ones who have expertise to assess how well the patient/client is doing and when she/he is ready to terminate treatment. These therapists do not respect the clinical judgment of the EAP professional and could jeopardize

future referrals. It is important to note that EAP professionals are privy to information not readily available to therapists, such as supervisor and colleague reports. A good
working relationship is enhanced when a therapist works
under the assumption that the EAP director has limited
resources to expend on psychotherapy. Indeed, the very
existence of these programs depends upon the administration of services in cost-efficient ways.

The EAP professional can be a reliable and interesting
source of referrals. In order to ensure success, the therapist
should keep the EAP professional informed on a regular
basis about the progress of the patient/client. This usually
can be done in the form of written updates that are brief, but
sufficiently detailed to describe progress, outcome, and
expected length of treatment. Some EAP professionals prefer periodic phone calls to discuss patient/client progress.
Other EAPs have designed their own procedures and forms
for collecting and reporting information. They are formatted
so the EAP professional can document the quality and quantity of their programs for management.

Michael Wakefield sees two major trends evolving with
EAPs. First, family issues will more and more dominate the
types of problems that present for assistance. Second, EAPs
will be much more involved with managed care. Therapists
will have to provide written documentation for all services
and will have to obtain preauthorization for blocks of session. EAP professionals should be able to advocate on
behalf of the patient/client and could make it easier to obtain
additional visits.

Question 41

How do I make sure I get paid for my work?

Answer

The easiest way to get paid is to require everyone to pay at the time services are rendered. Patients/clients are asked to file their own claims. Despite assertions of the opposite, very few private practitioners are able to operate in this way. This is because most patients/clients are accustomed to paying physicians co-payments rather than entire fees. Therefore, most patients/clients will choose a provider with whom they are compatible, including form of payment that is accepted. Consumers of mental health services are more likely to shop around. It is common now for these consumers to be price sensitive. "Price" of psychotherapy is not limited to the actual amount of the fee. It also includes a convenience element. Travel time, ease of parking, and acceptance of benefit assignment are factors that patients/clients consider in making choices.

Your responsibility as a business person is to inform the receptionist so that appropriate payment is collected for each patient/client leaving your office. Sometimes patients/clients just forget or are not sure what procedures they are supposed to follow. It is incumbent upon the therapist to address financial issues during the initial visit. Some therapists have difficulty addressing this issue. Most difficulties over fees can be resolved easily if they are addressed early. If they are allowed to go on for a while, it can interfere with the therapy process.

Question 42

How should I deal with delinquent accounts?

Answer

Even if you follow the advice we have provided to minimize difficulties with payments and collection of fees, there will still be occasions when patient accounts become delinquent. If many patient/client accounts are in arrears, and you have attempted to collect the debt, it may be time to conduct an audit of your business practices and modify your office management procedures accordingly.

After following the accepted collection procedures through repeated written statements and notices that the account is delinquent, you must then decide whether to write off the debt or seek assistance. If the debt is with a patient/client who is still in treatment, it is your responsibility to address this issue directly with the patient/client to determine if non-payment is of clinical significance. If there are transferential or other clinical issues, then it is clear you must address the failure to pay as a treatment issue.

In the event you cannot easily determine the patient/client's motives, it may be helpful to discuss the issue with a colleague. If the issues are not clearly clinical the best course of action is to discuss the problem with the patient/client and attempt to reach an agreement for making payments. Remember you cannot refuse to see a patient/client simply because money is owed to you. If you do, you could be guilty of *abandonment*, which is both unethical and illegal.

If the patient/client is no longer receiving services, you may not have the opportunity to address the debt therapeutically. It may be to your advantage to discuss the issue of nonpayment with the patient/client by phone and reach some mutually satisfactory accord. This may involve a demand for payment in full, establishing a payment schedule, reducing the fee, or even discharging the debt. As discussed by Woody (1989) in his book *Business Success in Mental Health Practice*, it may be useful to determine the potential risks and benefits when pursuing a bad debt. Although you may be able to collect all or part of a bad debt, it may cost you time and involve considerable aggravation. In addition, a debtor who is threatened with legal action may tell others about her/his displeasure with you. This could damage your reputation and may result in diminished referrals. Also, you are at increased risk of having a disgruntled former patient/client file a complaint about you to your professional association or licensing board. Even if unfounded, such a complaint requires you to spend your time and emotional energy. If you take the patient/client to court and actually win a judgment, it may be difficult or impossible to collect. Finally, even if you are successful in collecting the debt, it may be reduced substantially by the monetary costs of a collection agency or legal fees.

Question 43

What is a Fellow?

Answer

The greatest honor that a professional organization can bestow upon you is Fellowship status. It is the equivalent of being selected by the players to the all-star team. Only those individuals who have made a unique and/or distinguished contribution to their field are considered for fellowship status.

The practical application of this honor resides in its national status. Colleagues will feel more comfortable about making referrals to you from all over the country. You will be more likely to be asked to serve on committees that impact upon professional polices.

In psychology, the individual petitions the American Psychological Association for fellowship status through one of his/her member divisions. The candidate is sent an application and is asked to obtain three endorsers who have already achieved Fellowship status. The first screening is at the Division level. If the candidate passes, she/he is then nominated by the Division to a committee of the American Psychological Association, which reviews the application and recommendations to assure that the individual meets the standards. Once a member is accepted as a Fellow of APA, additional appointments to other divisions are much easier.

Question 44

Is it cost-effective for me to be a managed care provider?

Answer

Determination of cost-effectiveness in any of the work done by psychotherapists is very complex. The face of professional practice is changing very rapidly. In as much as managed care has supplanted indemnity insurance in terms of coverage of most people, it is unlikely that it will disappear in the next decade.

If you begin by determining how many hours per week you spend in professional activities that produce income, you have a basis to assess cost effectiveness. A starting point might be your last year or two years' practice. Now, calculate what proportion of these hours you receive your full UCR. Decide what percentage of your caseload are fee-for-service and what percentage are already discounted fees. Also, be sure to ascertain how much of your gross billing was noncollectible. Next, examine your records and compute how long it took to collect from third-party payers.

Now, you can decide how much time you have available in your schedule to see managed care referrals and how much net revenue is being collected. Since most managed care entities pay claims fairly quickly, your cash flow should improve if you increase your participation in managed care. There are other advantages to getting paid quickly you may not know. This is the *time value* of money concept which holds that today's money is more valuable than the same amount tomorrow because of inflation and the cost of credit. Thus, the $100 claim you collect this month is worth more than the $100 claim paid three months from now. If the money is rightfully yours now and is not paid to you for three months, you do not get the interest you would have gotten had the money been invested, nor will it go as far for consumer spending due to the effects of inflation.

The value of your professional time is determined by market forces; nobody but you can decide the value of your free time. You may prefer to spend an hour reading, going shopping, or just relaxing instead of seeing a managed care patient/client for a very reduced fee.

Question 45

What should be contained in practice brochures?

Answer

A brochure can be one of your best promotional tools. They must be inexpensive, succinct, and pleasing to the eye. It should also be consistent with your overall marketing plan and the image you want to project. To whom do you plan to target your brochures? Those for the general public should be different than those for referral agents. Similarly, those for school counselors will differ from brochures you might use with attorneys. For this reason, you may want to develop several different brochures.

Elements to be included in a brochure are as follows:

- Practice name, if you have one, and a logo—these make you distinctive.
- Your specialization or mission statement.
- Explanation of how or why your mission is needed or unique.
- Services that you provide.
- Practice location indicating directions and/or map and hours of operation.
- How to make referrals.
- Payments accepted—may include list of HMOs/PPOs accepted, if credit cards are accepted, accepting assignment of benefits, etc.
- List of professional staff—credentials, licenses, special interests, skills, and/or honors.

Question 46

How can I minimize patient/client record keeping?

Answer

Record-keeping becomes much less of a chore when you understand the reasons for doing so. Patient/client records are documentation that you have actually delivered the services for which you have contracted. Secondly, records document that you are making progress towards a therapeutic outcome. Thirdly, it is important to have a written history of the case in the event the patient/client transfers to another therapist. Finally, it is important to document that you have met standards of care in case liability issues should arise. If you have not documented appropriate actions on your part, it is assumed that you have been negligent.

Be as brief as possible in your patient/client notes. Long narratives can be misleading to a lay reader, such as the patient/client, and can be annoying to a busy professional. Some therapists develop checklists for case notes which can be completed in less than one or two minutes, yet meet all legal requirements. In the event a patient/client makes a statement threatening harm to self or another person, it is essential this be documented. Even if you have otherwise demonstrated exemplary professional behavior, you will be legally vulnerable if suicidal thoughts or behavior are not documented. There is an old maxim in medical record-keeping: "If it isn't written down, it didn't happen."

A final comment on the subject is for you to always be respectful of the patient/client in record-keeping and in communications with other professionals. Never record anything that is threatening to the patient/client's rights to his/her dignity. Remember, not only does the patient/client have the legal right to view his/her own clinical records, upon request, but the patient/client is a human being who had engaged you to perform professional work and is entitled to courteous, professional treatment in all spheres of your relationship.

Question 47

Why wasn't I taught anything about private practice management in graduate school? Is this going to change?

Answer

Historically, the scientist-practitioner model of training psychologists has been biased against professional practice, particularly in the private sector. Earlier generations of psychologists were employed in not-for-profit settings such as Veteran's Administration hospitals, public schools, community mental health centers, and universities. Similarly, other mental health professionals worked in various agencies that served mostly the poor or public, not-for-profit, settings. This started to change a decade or so ago when funding patterns for governmental and other publicly supported mental health programs shifted. Job opportunities for mental health professionals were no longer as abundant in the public and nonprofit sectors. In addition, with the advent of mandated mental health benefits in third-party payment plans there were increased demands for mental health providers to offer services in the private sector. Thus, it has only been in recent years that new graduates of mental health professional training programs have moved into private practice settings on a routine basis.

There had been significant controversy within academe about the overall curriculum with regard to incorporating business aspects of practice into training programs. This is not simply because academicians are unprepared by virtue of their lack of familiarity with the complexity of private practice, although this is certainly true. Rather, the body of knowledge involving theories, ethics, techniques, and so on, along with accreditation requirements have made it difficult for faculties to decide what to *exclude* from training yet feel they are doing a responsible job in preparing tomorrow's professionals. If everything faculty members wanted to include in the curriculum were included, some graduate training programs would double the length of time needed to complete all requirements. Nevertheless, because of the demands for preparing practitioners with a balanced education, graduate training programs are evolving and are now incorporating private practice management and economic issues into their curricula. This is advanced by the growing body of professional and scientific literature that has been produced over more than a decade. For those who did not receive training in practice management in their preservice education, it is necessary to acquire these skills on your own through reading the professional literature and attending workshops. But even if you did learn about the subject in graduate school, the field keeps changing and you still need to maintain and enhance your skills—not only about practice management, but in clinical areas as well.

Question 48

What is the role and best use of computers in private practice?

Answer

Computers are valuable tools for a variety of purposes in professional practices. A recent survey, reported in *Practice Strategies* (Anon., 1997), found that over two-thirds of all private practitioners owned or used computers in their practices. David Adams, Ph.D., of Atlanta, has made creative use of computer technology for many years. He outlines six major categories of utilization for which commercially available software can be obtained easily:

1. Diagnosis and assessment
2. Accounting and billing
3. Database management
4. Word processing
5. Statistics
6. Communication and networking

There is a burgeoning business in the development and distribution of software to both administer and score psychological tests. In fact, some have been developed that can only be administered and scored with the aid of a computer. Many of the tests commonly used in clinical practice for assessment of intelligence, mood, and personality (e.g., WAIS, WISC, Beck Depression Inventory, MMPI, Rorschach) are available for computer scoring and interpretation, including preparation of narrative reports. In addition, diagnostic aids for clinician use and the entire DSM-IV are available on disk for use with desktop or notebook computers.

Accounting and billing software, and those used for database management used to be available for only large scale operations. Now, they are relatively inexpensive and within the reach of clinicians who are in solo practice on a part-time basis. Several software providers specialize in mental health applications. Programs that assist in establishing goals and treatment plans are helpful in working with managed care patients/clients because of the time-saving feature.

Word processing presents a different set of judgments. If your practice includes many psychological evaluations or reports, and/or you communicate regularly with referral sources, a word processing package can save money on secretarial time. It can also effectively and neatly organize and produce communications (such as newsletters) which can enhance your professional image and reduce marketing costs.

Statistical and networking software are used by the sophisticated "hacker" and for specialized purposes. Those clinicians who are interested in research and comparing their data with other research centers will need a statistical package, such as SPSS or StatSoft (1-918-749-1119). Also, with the growth of the internet there is plenty of opportunity to communicate with other mental health professionals around the world. It is amazing how many newsgroups of varying specialties have sprung up and can be contacted through e-mail. There are even professional journals that are distributed directly through e-mail. This is an easy way to keep abreast of changes, advances, and current issues much more rapidly than the era of print-only communication.

Recently, programs have come on the market that are useful adjuncts to psychotherapy in actual clinical practice. They have undergone a major evolution since ELIZA, the well-known psychotherapy simulation developed by Joseph Weizenbaum in the 1960s. Programs are now commercially available for stress management, cognitive modification, building self-esteem, and relaxation training, among others. A commercial resource for some therapeutic programs is Multi-Health Systems, Inc. (1-800-456-3003). There are also numerous written resources which discuss uses of computers in therapy, such as Marc Schwartz's *Using Computers in Clinical Practice* (1984). Naturally, while useful as adjuncts to therapy, these programs are not intended to be replacements for therapy performed by a qualified psychotherapist. This is an ideal, of course, and we can only speculate how these tools may be misapplied by bottom line-oriented MCO managers.

Question 49

Why can't I deduct uncollected bills from my income taxes?

Answer

Unlike manufacturing businesses, mental health providers and other service businesses have somewhat unique characteristics. Since service businesses are on cash, rather than accrual tax bases, tax is paid only on money that is collected, minus legitimate deductions. In a sense, uncollected bills are "written off" when the actual amount collected is accounted for in the income category on Schedule C. In short, by not paying tax on what was billed, but only on what was collected, you did write off the part that you did not collect.

Question 50

Should I serve as an expert witness?

Answer

The answer is dependent, of course, on the depth of your experience and your ability to choose clients well. An expert witness is a person who can provide testimony that is due to his/her having professional training or knowledge. In essence, this means that you must know what you are talking about and can project expertise. As an example, if you have not had specialized training in neuropsychology you might not want to seriously consider testifying in a head injury case. If you do not have credentials or documented experience as either a child or family therapist, you might want to pass on a child custody case.

Expert witnesses must be prepared to answer questions at both depositions and trials. In a deposition you will be asked questions about the case by an opposing lawyer whose duty it is to dispute or even discredit your testimony. Since you cannot prepare for all of his/her questions, you must be both knowledgeable and articulate. At the trial your deposition will be used by the opposing attorney to present arguments for his/her client's case. Once again, you will have no prior knowledge of the questions you will be asked during your testimony, or of the manner the attorney will use your own words from your deposition to refute your statements. You *must* know what you are talking about and present your findings and/or opinions in a manner that is understandable to the judge and jury, if there is one.

Psychologist and attorney Bob Woody (1991) maintains that mental health providers have a duty to make their skills available to the legal system. Yet, he points to risks that go beyond the bruised egos and emotional beatings that may be suffered at the hands of opposing attorneys, namely financial ones. A major risk of working as an expert witness is that you will not be paid. The expert witness is in line, after the lawyer, for payment by the client. Normally, severe financial obligations are placed on the litigants, which may mean that you stand to be underpaid, or not paid at all.

A second risk is that you might also be sued. People who sue others are a greater risk for suing you. Despite these considerations, many psychotherapists choose to be expert witnesses because of the challenge and potential monetary rewards. Woody advises anyone pursuing forensic work to heed six guidelines:

1. Consider every client a potential litigant.
2. Do not allow yourself to be used as a "fact" witness by attorneys. If you render a professional opinion you *are* a professional witness and entitled to a professional fee.
3. Inform clients of your forensic fee policy in writing from the onset of your professional relationship.
4. When litigation is near, secure a written contractual obligation for payment from the client.
5. Be selective in the cases you accept and avoid those who are high risk for nonpayment (e.g., those with severe personality disorders).

REFERENCES

Anon. (1990). Managed care: Here are 39 major companies that want your services. *Psychotherapy Finances, 16*(12), 3-7.

Anon. (1990). Fee and practice survey highlights. *Psychotherapy Finances, 16*(14), whole issue.

Anon. (1996). Private practice: Fees, incomes and trends. *Practice Strategies, 2*(12), whole issue.

Anon. (1997). Three MCOs control industry as consolidation speeds up. *Practice Strategies, 3*(9), 1,4.

Anon. (1997) Practice fee, incomes and trends report. *Practice Strategies, 3* (12), whole issue.

Bennett, B. E., Bryant, B. K., Vandenbos, G. R., & Greenwood, A. (1990). *Professional liability and risk management.* Washington, DC: American Psychological Association.

Cummings, N. A. (1991). Ten ways to spot mismanaged mental health. *Psychotherapy in Private Practice, 9.*

DeLeon, P. H., Fox, R. E., & Graham, S. R. (1991). Prescription privileges: Psychology's next frontier? *American Psychologist, 46*, 384-393.

Forman, B. D. (1990). Media, marketing & psychology. *Psychotherapy Bulletin, 25*, 34.

Forman, B. D. (1990/91). Let's make psychology safe for malpractice. *Psychotherapy Bulletin, 25*, 17.

Forman, B. D. & Forman, K. S. (1987). *Fundamentals of marketing the private psychotherapy practice.* Springfield, IL: Charles C Thomas, Publisher.

Lowry, J. L. & Ross, M. J. (1997). Expectations of psychotherapy duration: How long should psychotherapy last? *Psychotherapy, 34*, 272-277.

Phillips, E. L. (1987). The ubiquitous decay curve: Service delivery similarities in psychotherapy, medicine, and addiction. *Professional Psychology: Research and Practice, 18*, 650-652.

Pope, K. S. (1989). Malpractice suits, licensing disciplinary actions, and ethics cases: Frequencies, causes, and costs. *The Independent Practitioner, 9*, 22-26.

Schwartz, M. D. (Ed.) (1984). *Using computers in clinical practice.* New York: Haworth.

Small, R. F. (1991). *Maximizing third-party reimbursement in your mental health practice.* Sarasota, FL: Professional Resource Exchange.

Turkington, C. (1986). Suit data show no need to panic. *American Psychological Association Monitor, 17,* 9.

VandeCreek, L. (1990). Claims made/occurrence based professional liability policies. *Psychotherapy Bulletin, 25,* 35-37.

Woody, R. H. (1988). *Fifty ways to avoid malpractice: A guidebook for mental health professionals.* Sarasota, FL: Professional Resource Exchange.

Woody, R. H. (1989). *Business Success in Mental Health Practice.* San Francisco: Jossey-Bass.

Woody, R. H. (1991). Financial safeguards in forensic psychology cases. *The Florida Psychologist, 41*(3), 10-12.